Shards of Solace

Esosa Frances Mohammed

BookLeaf Publishing

India | USA | UK

Presentation by *BookLeaf Publishing*

Web: www.bookleafpub.com

E-mail: info@bookleafpub.com

ISBN: 9789360946197

First edition 2024

*To Pip, the one who inspired these verses.
You are the muse breathing life into each
stanza.*

ACKNOWLEDGEMENT

I would like to thank BookLeaf Publishing for the opportunity to share my work with others in this way.

PREFACE

I poured my heart onto these pages as a means of cathartic self-exploration, trying to make sense of love's euphoric highs and devastating lows through verse. By expressing the raw emotions of heartbreak, grief, and the tender process of finding hope and healing, I aspired to create a resonant collection that could serve as a lighthouse for others adrift in similar turbulent waters.

When we open ourselves to love, we unavoidably invite both beauty and pain. In this collection, I have painstakingly carved verses from the depths of my soul, documenting a journey through love's exhilarating arrival, gut-wrenching loss, and the extraordinarily complex process of finding the strength to go on.

These poems are profoundly personal, yet their collective essence is undeniably universal. They give voice to the piercing wounds, hollowing emptiness, restless despair, and emotional rebirth experienced during different periods of our lives.

More than anything, this book lays bare the resilience of the human heart - its incredible capacity to emerge from devastation. I invite you to trace each curve of healing within these lines, and perhaps find solace in knowing you are never alone when navigating loss. After all, though love and heartache are oceans we separately brave, the endless tides connect us all.

For those whose hearts have ever been shattered, may you find solace in knowing you're not alone on this path. To the dreamers still seeking their twin flame, may love's poetry keep you afloat.

Echoes of the Unspoken

Our thoughts stay silent, never making a sound
Our minds, oftentimes in a whirlpool of
emotions and turmoil, rages on, silently and
steadily in anguish, charting its course through
the stretch
Our tears, running down softly, can be tasted but
make no sound.

Our hearts, broken and hurting, echo no
resonance
No outward portrayal of the inner agony and
pain we undergo or of the piercing Ache we
experience when nighttime comes and we are all
alone
Weary, hurting, trying to smile through it all
with elegance.

Where memories whisper of what once we
shared and relished
With nightfall comes a deafening silence, a void
Love's imprint remains, a haunting refrain
Each breath drawn is a tense reminder of the loss
we have sustained.

Though dawn breaks through, darkness persists

A numbing cocoon where the soul exists.
The world carries on with its clamor and sound
Yet our hearts remain muted by heartache's
staggering depths.

Scorched Heartland

The pain was too much to bear
The hurt too much to live with
Her heart a barren wasteland, scorched and
battered
Tears became the only rain to quench this
blazing fire
Would she be able to get past this phase of her
life?
It seemed almost impossible
The love she had counted on was no more
The future she dreamt of was gone
All she had left was a past she could not face
She did not want to know what lay in store for
her
So she buried her face in her pillow and cried
To what end or purpose?
None, for it would take a lake, a river, an ocean
to wash away her pain.

Unreal Realities

It is there
Constantly lurking
Mocking even
An air of the unreal that steadfastly refuses to
retreat
Day and night
All around
It clings to my actions and penetrates my
thoughts
What is this?
Why is this?
Yet there lies no answers in mere rhetoric
At night, sleep eludes me
And if by a stroke of luck, blessed sleep creeps
and drops on my eyelid,
It is not long before I come awake again
Pray tell, what do I wake to?
Not tangibility
Not normalcy
Not even a moment of respite
But then it would seem that while I was asleep, I
was at peace.

Solitude Adrift

I was lost in a world of my own
Sailing in no direction at all
Unable to comprehend why I was here
What I was here for.
I felt tears sting my eyes
And a lump form in my throat
I wanted to cry out and tell the world the pain I
bore in silence,
But there was no one to talk to, no one to
understand,
I closed my eyes and prayed, "Lead me Lord,"
And immediately, I felt at ease once again as
though a heavy burden had been Lifted off, and I
was now back to myself
Someone I had never known or understood.

Love's Whispered Farewell

Why do I hurt
Why do I cry
Why does my heart ache so
Maybe it is because I lost what I never truly had
Or that the world had suddenly grown hollow
Or as it feels like an essential plug had been
pulled inside of me
Memories haunt me, of your warm embrace
Love's sweet whispers now echoes of the past
Shattered pieces scatter the floor
Tears fall like rain
A heart once whole, now broken to the core
Time's gentle hand may mend and heal,
But the scars of heartbreak, forever I will feel.

The Last Shred of Self

I gazed up, shocked and bewildered
"Nooooooo," I screamed out loudly and
instinctively
I knew if I stayed facing that cruel person
I would begin to howl in an outrageous, indecent
pain.

So, I sat there motionless, my chest tight,
constricted
The depth of betrayal was such that
It was impossible to immediately comprehend
My humiliation was quite complete.

My eyes misted over with tears as I walked
away
Taking with me the one thing I still owned
My dignity, a tattered mantle,
Threadbare and worn, was all I had left.

A Single Path

Why? Why?
I wanted to scream out the words
But they remained locked up inside me
Like the panic I refused to acknowledge.
Discovering I had been living and loving a lie
Hit me like a bolt of lightning
Shook me to the core
I had discovered in one flash
a cruelty, a ruthlessness the size of which
I could only begin to imagine
There I stood, helpless and powerless
In an arena where there could be no victory
An arena from which there
could be no escape except an honorable retreat.

Reverie's Bitter Awakening

Cautiously, she allowed the floodgate of her
emotions to open
And it all seemed like a badly written scene in
which she must play.

Confusion whirled around her mind at the ordeal
she faced.
She felt like a prey, trapped by her own naivety.
Was her angel a fallen angel?

Coming out of her reverie,
She could still feel the silence that now pervaded
her spirit.

A terrible stillness born out of those scathing
words of betrayal.
Taking a deep breath, she is suddenly allowed an
insight into an existing truth.

All her life seemed to take shape and
contradictions melted away.
Her angel really was a fallen angel.

Stirrings Through Grief's Shroud

What is this that absorbs me totally and
completely?
This thing that steals my senses and draws my
breath?
What is this that shuts my sight, tugs at my
heart, and draws my spirit?
From shadowed depths where sorrow dwelled
A flicker stirred; a light first felled
But slowly, softly, it began to burn
Against the shroud of endless grey
Hope's resilience held stubborn sway
Through the shroud of grief, a tender glow
Emerged to thaw through my wall of sorrow and
woe.

A reminder that darkness is conceived
To be by dawning rays relieved
A hopeful spark amidst the gloom
To lead from despondency's grasp
As hope's warm radiance lit my way
And pierced the gloom with hopeful view
I watched new possibilities arise
No longer trapped in sorrow's knell
But fueled by light's eternal swell
The fragile seedling, light rebound.

Journey of Resilience

Relentless spirit, unbroken, unbound,
Emerging stronger from trials profound.
Setbacks and struggles become stepping stones,
Inspiring courage where fear had once grown.
Laying gently, doubt and despair that bar the
way,
Igniting hope with each newfound day.
Embracing challenges with grit and grace,
Never retreating, steadfast in pace.
Conquering doubts, rising above,
Emboldened by faith, fortified by love.

Resilience shines like a beacon bright,
Lightening paths through the darkest night.
Steadfast and sturdy, rooted yet malleable,
Innately equipped to confront all that is
assailable.
Leaving adversity weary, waning,
Indomitable spirit always remaining.
Endeavoring onwards, fueled by resolve,
Never stagnant, always evolving.
Crafting new stories, new trajectories to pursue,
Etching resilience in all that she does.

Memories Etched in Time

Just like ships that pass in the night,
Our paths crossed and from that moment onward
There was no mountain high enough.

I was startled by the depth of my feelings which
seemed almost ethereal.
I reveled in my happiness.
Golden memories were made just by being
together and it all felt so right.

I strive to recall every moment we have spent
together,
Every gesture, smile, laughter, every word I
treasure.
You are truly a part of my most treasured
memories that time cannot erase.

Endless Wellspring

For some, it is fleeting, perhaps a whiff, or even
a song
While for others it is concrete, tangible, and
reachable.
For a long time, I struggled to recognize what
mine was
A smile, a touch, a voice?

I pondered all through the night, the day, and in
between
What if I never had any, a little voice whispered
to me
Maybe it is a myth that many have intimated,
but in reality, does not exist
Simply because that allusion defies all
understanding.

Yet as I daydreamed, I was filled with tingles
and memories
Each one becoming more vivid as my eyes
Opened to my bedrock of strength
When I was sure I could not go on.

Faith held me together, glued my heart that was
seemingly broken into tiny pieces. Its gentle

force a beacon, guiding me through the darkest
valleys.
Friendships with kindred spirits, a balm for my
soul, banding together to dispel Sorrow's heavy
burdens.
Family, an unbreakable bond, a sheltering tree,
Roots intertwined, branches embracing, together
we are stronger.
Laughter, the magic elixir that cures all ills,
Chasing shadows away, filling the heart until it
trills.
Curiosity, that endless wellspring, forever
replenished
Fueling the hunger to learn, to live, every
moment relished
Memories, always close, never far, lured and
beckoned to me with a twinkle.

Superpowers of mine, I cherish you so dearly
For in you, I find reservoirs of fortitude to brave
each gale.
Family, faith, friendship, and laughter,
You are my light, my compass, you never fail.

A Spirit Ignited

A quiet flame burning slowly but steadfastly
through the darkness, putting doubts to shame
Infusing her with the ability to rise, to adapt, to
grow
To embrace life's challenges, letting hope flow
It lifts her spirit, letting her reach for the sky
Paving the way for her to craft a vibrant life,
come what may
Not a force to wield, but a strength to believe
It lies in the courage to face each new day
And find beauty in the journey, come what may
The extraordinary in the ordinary untold
The strength to keep going, to cherish every
breath
Embracing each moment, until her final rest.

Fate's Tapestry

October, poignant reminder, forever etched, I reminisce,
Our pip days, which I forever miss.
As I drift, my compass unsure,
I grasp for the brilliance of your smile.
I see your essence in each crimson maple leaf,
Reminiscent of the joy that once filled us with delight and pure joy.
Love of mine, your beauty divine,
Yet in this poignant moment, I find solace in the truth,
That your essence lives on, a timeless, ageless proof,
Treasuring what was and what now remains.

Rays of Sunshine (An Ode to the Tetrad)

O precious gems, my tetradic wonder, so
beloved,
Like rays of brilliant sunshine, you shine,
Illuminating my world with boundless love,
Pure blessings sent from the heavens above.

My eldest child, my wise and noble guide,
Your strength and courage fill my heart with
pride.
My second-born, with charm and high energy,
melodious ring,
Your quiet strength and wisdom take wing.

Sweet middle child, with compassion's gentle
embrace,
In your exquisite humor, solace I can trace.
My youngest babe, our family's shining star,
Lighting our path through ups and downs afar.

Together you four, a fine tapestry divine,
Each thread distinct, yet brilliantly entwined.
Our life's greatest joys, our richest treasures,
In your splendid beings, love knows no measure.

O darling children, diamonds precious and true,
Forever you will be our most cherished smiles,
Each one as fresh as the morning dew
The brightest stars in our eternal skies.

My Angel Born Asleep – A Sonnet

My precious child, you left before we met,
Torn from this world in childbirth's tragic night.
Though in my arms you laid fleetingly yet,
You will forever shine most radiant light.

I dreamed of you, a face of purest grace,
Gazing into eyes that twinkled and sparkled with
dreams and lively delight.
With a mother's love, I longed to know each
trace,
Of your tiny lips, sweet cheeks, and soft raven
hair as dark as night.

Yet fate decreed you would not stay,
And you slipped to God's eternal keep.
My arms, heart, and eyes still ache to feel your
warmth so sweet,
While in my heart, your presence evermore I
will keep.

These fourteen lines, a vessel for my anguish
Of sentiments too deep for me to share.

Steadfast and Unwavering

For my worth, my treasure is the only thing I
truly know.
A priceless jewel that shines from my heart's
deepest corners,
Not measured by wealth or affluence,
But by the strength of my spirit and the lessons
life has given.

My worth is forged in the fires of adversity,
Tempered by challenges that shape my resolve,
Reminding me that resilience is a vital necessity,
And within my heart, true grit will forever
evolve.

It is the compass that guides me through doubt's
shadowy maze,
The armor that shields me from the world's
harsh judgments,
Empowering me to walk with confidence,
ablaze,
Embracing my flaws as unique embellishments.

As I encounter highs and lows, wade through
tumultuous and tranquil moments,

My worth remains a constant, steadfast, and
unwavering story
Of self-acceptance, resilience, and the choice to
be,
Celebrating the miraculous essence of just being
me.

A Tapestry of Fine Purpose

Her greatest fear?
The torture of drifting, lackluster living, lacking
passion, desire, or yearning
Each day an empty canvas unable to fill
Her brushstrokes devoid of any purpose and will
The thought of never gaining a chance to create
or explore
The whisper of being stuck overwhelms,
threatening to overpower the mind.

Yet she knows each day presents an open page
A blank canvas for her to engage
With actions designed from purposeful strokes
Painting a legacy of undiscovered strength and
resilience.

Spreading more light in a world running wild
Being a beacon in humanity's long night.

It is found in the smile you bestow
On a weary stranger's furrowed brow
In tending the sick, holding space with those
who grieve
It blossoms in standing for truth
Forging bonds between strangers as kin

Tearing down walls that would shut others out.

A life worth living honors the sweat and pain
Tears and joy, dreams and realities.
It blossoms in the winter and tethers in the
spring.
It weaves in fought battles for justice and right,
Shielding the meek from oppression's cold
plight.
A life with true meaning crafts human ties.
It undertakes quests of growth evermore.
An insatiable hunger to unlock wisdom's doors,
Sharing that knowledge like watering seeds
Helping more blossoms unfurl from their life's
needs.
A life worth living is truly a life well done.

Becoming

Blossoming from the seed of potential
Emerging slowly, steadily, reverential
Casting off self-limiting beliefs
Opening to truths and experiences' own elegance
that bring relief
Molting layers of fear and doubt
Inviting the birthright of courage out
Nurturing the growth before unseen
Gratefully unfolding at nature's wise pace while
I embrace this life serene.

Buoyed by the currents of persistence and
perseverance
Evolving in strength, each challenge a
tantalizing invitation
Climbing ever higher, vision expanding
Obstacles traverse, no dream too demanding
Magnificently rising, resounding, alive
Inhabited by the strength that I have learned to
revive
Navigating the grim yet rewarding path of
self-discovery
Reveling, even daring to sparkle in the radiance.
I am becoming.

Life's Miraculous Gifts

Bound by blood, forged under one family tree
Our childhood, a vibrant tapestry of friendship,
fights, and laughter
Filled with colors too numerous to describe
With tales and anecdotes only siblings could
ever fathom or comprehend.

From red dust playgrounds and skies indigo
To cherry and emerald trees swaying in
evening's glow
Our youthful days echoed the rhythms of nurture
and home
Anchored in bonds that could weather any
storm.

Through the great dynamics of connectedness
Trading dreams and stories untold of Odo and
Lapote
We journey side-by-side, our kinship unfurls
with every stage of our lives
Forming a sequence of hearts against the wide,
often bewildering world.

Now, though cities and oceans may part and
separate

One truth remains, our connection grows
unchanged
Refusing to be drawn apart, we take each other's
hands
Grateful for the bond that holds steadfastly and
unwavering.

I am

I am from sub-Saharan Africa, home to
hundreds of languages, cultures, and ethnicities.
From masquerades, festivals, folklore, and
soulful music that taught me about the history,
heritage, and traditions in which I was raised.

I am from dry, scorching heat that softly and
sweetly tingles my skin as I travel through the
city. From tropical seasons that quickly usher in
the increasingly tempestuous yet melodious rain.
From the dry harmattan season that can only be
compared to verdant landscapes with its dry,
rasping caress.

I am from a land filled with ample respect
instilled from a young age which today serves as
my bedrock to respect and revere ALL people
and ALL viewpoints irrespective of color,
gender, income, education, and class. From
truth, justice, and tolerance emanating from my
ethnic roots and connecting to my identity as a
woman, a mother, a daughter, a sister, a friend,
and a native of the world.

I am from Sweet and Felix, the best and finest
who teach me what it truly means to be strong
yet vulnerable, to be kind yet firm, to love
myself, and to be true to who I am. From
childhood breakfasts of beanballs to afternoon
meals of jollof rice and plantain to evening
delicacies of suya and onions.

I am from the comfort and solace of Psalm 91
which assures me that the Lord is my refuge and
fortress and that he will deliver me from the
snare of the fowler. From the promises of Psalm
23 that reassure me that goodness and love will
follow me all the days of my life.

I am from pain, grief, trauma, and heartache that
etches across the seat of my mind but also from
love, tenderness, strength, and unbridled joy
buoyed by an anchor line to joy's haven held
fast. From roots paradoxically seeped in anguish
and bliss.

I am from family, friendship, faith, and
forgiveness which enable me to overcome
adversity and strife, bringing me healing and
restoration.

www.ingramcontent.com/pod-product-compliance
Lightning Source LLC
LaVergne TN
LVHW010952200726

843509LV00013B/2389